REALLY WEIRD ANIMALS

CLARE HIBBERT

W
FRANKLIN WATTS
LONDON • SYDNEY

First published in paperback i▮

First published in 2011 by Fra▮

Copyright © Arcturus Holdings Limited

Franklin Watts
338 Euston Road
London NW1 3BH

Franklin Watts Australia
Level 17/207 Kent Street, Sydney NSW 2000

Produced by Arcturus Publishing Limited,
26/27 Bickels Yard, 151–153 Bermondsey Street, London SE1 3HA

Series concept: Discovery Books Ltd, 2 College Street, Ludlow, Shropshire SY8 1AN
www.discoverybooks.net

Managing editor: Paul Humphrey
Editor: Clare Hibbert
Design: sprout.uk.com
Picture researcher: Laura Durman

Photo acknowledgements: Corbis: p 17 (Carol Hughes/Gallo Images); FLPA: pp 8 (Hugh Lansdown), 14 (Michael & Patricia Fogden/Minden Pictures), 15 (Michael & Patricia Fogden/Minden Pictures), 21 (Mitsuhiko Imamori/Minden Pictures); Getty Images: cover and pp 1 (Anthony Bannister/Gallo Images), 12 (David Maitland), 18 (Heidi & Hans-Jurgen Koch/Minden Pictures); iStockphoto: pp 27t (Paul Tessier), 28t (andrewwongcs), 29 (jeridu); Dr Jeremy Miller: p 4; Oxford Scientific Films: p 6 (Densey Clyne); Photoshot: pp 5b (Stephen Dalton), 7 (James Carmichael Jr), 11t (Daniel Heuclin), 11b (Photo Researchers), 13 (David Maitland), 19 (James Carmichael Jr), 20 (Photo Researchers), 22 (ANT), 23 (Ken Griffiths), 25t (Nick Garbutt); Shutterstock Images: pp 3 (Basel101658), 5t (exOrzist), 9 (Emran Mohd Tamil), 10 (Audrey Snider-Bell), 16 (Basel101658), 24t (D&K Kucharscy), 24b (Christian Musat), 25b (Evgeniy Ayupov), 26t (Ivan Kuzmin), 26b (Judy Whitton), 27b (orionmystery@flickr), 28b (orionmystery@flickr), 31 (Emran Mohd Tamil), 32 (D&K Kucharscy).

Cover picture: A wolf spider.

A CIP catalogue record for this book is available from the British Library.

Dewey Decimal Classification Number 595.4'4

ISBN 978 1 4451 3820 6
SL001746UK

Printed in China

Franklin Watts is a division of Hachette Children's Books, an Hachette UK company.
www.hachette.co.uk

CONTENTS

ASSASSIN SPIDER

The assassin spider's jaws are a lethal weapon. They are super-long, so the spider can hold its struggling victim away from its body, while it injects venom from its fangs.

ASSASSIN SPIDER FACTS

SIZE: 2-mm-long body
HOME: forests in Australia, South Africa and Madagascar
EATS: other arachnids

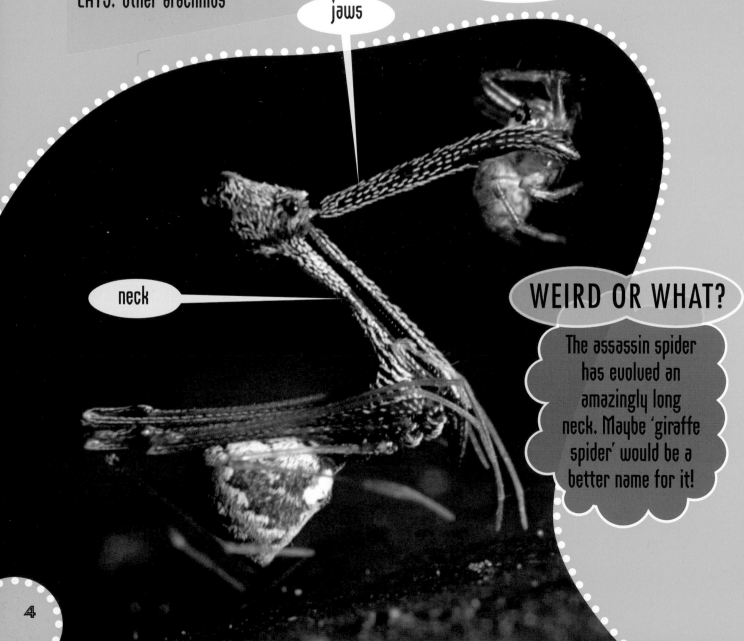

jaws

neck

WEIRD OR WHAT?

The assassin spider has evolved an amazingly long neck. Maybe 'giraffe spider' would be a better name for it!

Everyone knows that spitting is a disgusting habit. But for the slow-moving spitting spider, it's the best way to get a meal.

SPITTING SPIDER

WEIRD OR WHAT?

The spider can target its prey from a distance of more than 1 centimetre – that may not sound much, but it's about twice its own body length!

The spider spits a blob of glue and venom at its victim so it can't move. Together they stick the prey to the spot and then paralyze it. This spider's just immobilized a mosquito and it's moving in for the kill.

SPITTING SPIDER FACTS

SIZE: 6-mm-long body
HOME: worldwide
EATS: insects (eg mosquitoes, house flies)

5

BOLAS SPIDER

BOLAS SPIDER FACTS

SIZE: females have 15-mm bodies;
       males are 2 mm across
HOME: America, Africa and
       Australasia
EATS: moths or moth flies

Bolas spiders are the gauchos of the arachnid world. Instead of making a web, the spider spins a silken bolas with a sticky blob at the end. It swings this towards its prey and Wham! it's caught its lunch!

This bolas spider, called a magnificent spider, lives in Australia. It is dangling its lasso to snare a passing moth.

6

There are more than 60 species of bolas spider. Most are picky eaters who feed on one particular moth species.

WEIRD OR WHAT?

A bolas spider has an amazing trick for luring the right kind of male moths. It produces pheromones - the special scent that female moths give off to attract a mate!

On average, a female bolas spider catches a couple of moths a night. By day she rests – and depends on camouflage to save her from predators.

SPINY ORB WEAVER

The spiny orb weaver wins the prize for being the punkiest spider. Its body is circled by spikes! Some spiders have six spikes; others as many as ten!

SPINY ORB WEAVER FACTS

SIZE: body up to 3 cm long
HOME: temperate and tropical forests
EATS: whiteflies, flies, moths, beetles

The spikes – and the bright colours – help to put off forest birds that might be tempted to snack on the spider.

This unusual looking spiny orb weaver has a pair of long horns. It lives in the Malaysian rainforest.

The spider decorates its web with little tufty bits of silk. No one is sure why – maybe it's to make the web more visible to birds that might crash into it.

WEIRD OR WHAT?

Male spiny orb weavers don't have spikes. They have four or five little humps on their back instead.

GOLIATH BIRD-EATING SPIDER

The goliath bird-eater is the world's biggest, scariest, hairiest spider! The size of a dinner plate, it's a kind of tarantula that lives in the Amazon rainforest.

WEIRD OR WHAT?

When threatened, a goliath bird-eater rubs its hairy legs together to produce a loud hissing noise. The sound can be heard 5 metres away!

Yikes! This bird-eater has raised its front legs and is about to strike.

BIRD-EATING SPIDER FACTS

SIZE: 30-cm leg span
HOME: South American rainforest
EATS: invertebrates, small reptiles, birds and mammals

This spider's dragged a chick from its nest. The goliath bird-eater has also been known to eat rats, bats, lizards and snakes. More usually, though, it makes a meal of insects and other invertebrates.

Check out these fangs! They can be nearly 4 centimetres long. They are used to inject paralyzing venom into prey.

NET-CASTING SPIDER

Forget hanging around on a web hoping for prey! The net-casting spider uses its spinning skills to weave a rectangular net. Then it lies in wait, holding the net in its four front legs.

NET-CASTING SPIDER FACTS

SIZE: females are about 2 cm long
HOME: tropical areas worldwide
EATS: insects

When an insect walks by, the spider traps it in the stretchy net. It can catch flying insects too, by flicking the net into the air.

The net-casting spider is sometimes nicknamed the ogre-faced spider because of its pair of scary, outsize eyes!

The net's not sticky, but it's made from such a tangle of threads that it's almost impossible to escape from.

The net-casting spider is a night hunter. Two of its eight eyes are much bigger than the rest and these give it excellent night vision.

CAMEL SPIDER

A camel spider relies on speed to run down its prey. It can scuttle along at 16 kilometres per hour – that's about five times faster than the sprinting speed of most spiders, and about the same speed as a human runner!

WEIRD OR WHAT?

Camel spiders can make a rattling sound by rubbing together their mouthparts. Like a rattlesnake's rattle, the noise scares off would-be predators.

Camel spiders are not true spiders, but they belong to the same class of animals: the arachnids. Other non-spider arachnids include harvestmen and scorpions.

All arachnids have eight legs. Camel spiders appear to have ten, but the front pair are sense organs, a bit like an insect's antennae.

Camel spiders are desert dwellers, which is how they got their name. The sight of a camel spider would certainly make you watch your step in the sand.

CAMEL SPIDER FACTS

SIZE: 7-cm-long body and 12-cm leg span
HOME: deserts or dry grasslands worldwide except Australia
EATS: arthropods (eg termites, darkling beetles), small lizards

FISHING

Fishing spiders have a crafty way of catching food. They lurk on the bank of a pond or stream, resting a foot or two on the water.

When a fishing spider senses ripples, it races across the surface of the water to catch the passing insect or fish.

FISHING SPIDER FACTS

SIZE: the largest females have a leg span of 8 cm

HOME: near fresh water, almost worldwide

EATS: aquatic insects (eg mayflies, pond skaters), fish, frogs

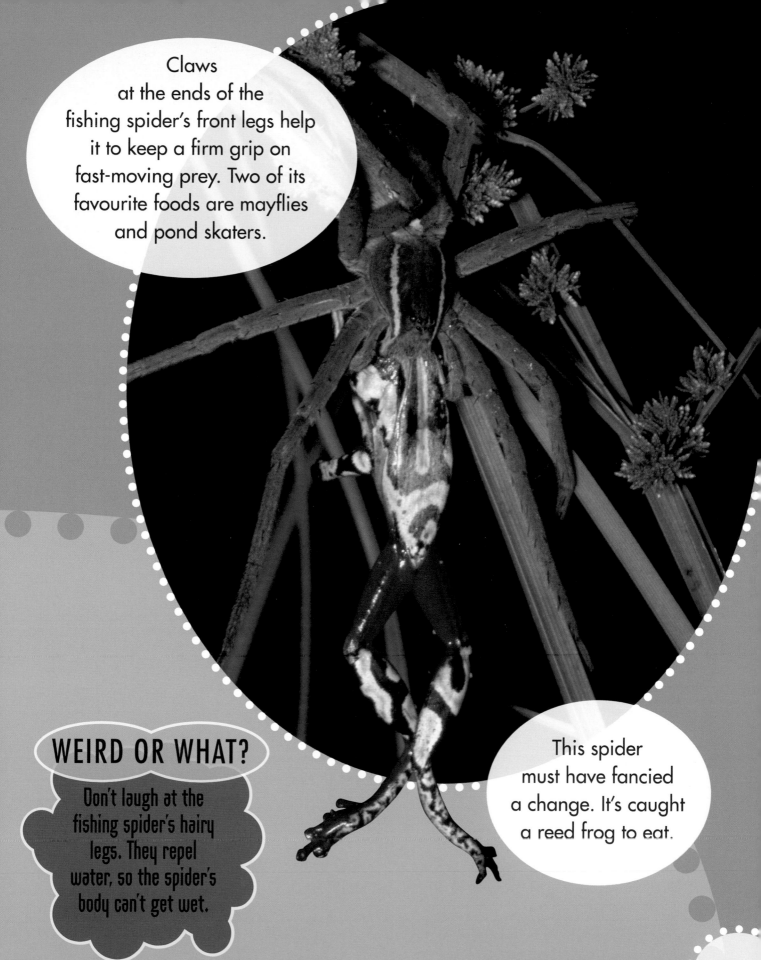

Claws at the ends of the fishing spider's front legs help it to keep a firm grip on fast-moving prey. Two of its favourite foods are mayflies and pond skaters.

WEIRD OR WHAT?

Don't laugh at the fishing spider's hairy legs. They repel water, so the spider's body can't get wet.

This spider must have fancied a change. It's caught a reed frog to eat.

DIVING-BELL SPIDER

DIVING-BELL SPIDER FACTS

Diving-bell spiders spend their lives underwater. They spin themselves a bell-shaped home and fill it with air – just like a mini submarine!

SIZE: 1-cm-long body
HOME: freshwater ponds in Europe, northern Asia and north Africa
EATS: aquatic insect larvae, water fleas, *Cyclops* (tiny crustaceans)

WEIRD OR WHAT?

The male diving-bell spider spins a tunnel linking his own diving bell to his mate's!

When air in the bell starts to run out, the spider lets the bell bob back to the surface and collects more bubbles.

The dewdrop spider gets its name from its silvery markings, which make its body look like a shining drop of dew.

DEWDROP SPIDER

DEWDROP SPIDER FACTS

SIZE: 4-mm-long body
(though some species are 1 cm)
HOME: tropics
EATS: tiny insects

This cheeky spider doesn't bother to spin its own web. Instead, it sets up home on a bigger spider's web, and steals its prey.

WEIRD OR WHAT?

Having a dewdrop spider as a squatter isn't necessarily a nuisance. The spider helps its host by clearing away small prey and keeping the web neat and tidy.

TRAPDOOR SPIDER

This sneaky spider lives in a burrow. The entrance to its underground lair is a perfectly camouflaged, silk-hinged door. All day, the spider sits in its burrow … and waits.

Spreading out from the door are silken trip wires. If an unsuspecting insect stumbles over one, it alerts the spider. It darts out of the trapdoor to seize its prey.

TRAPDOOR SPIDER FACTS

SIZE: 2.5-cm-long body
HOME Americas, Europe, Asia
EATS: insects (eg crickets,
grasshoppers, beetles),
other spiders, small lizards

Like most spiders,
the trapdoor spider uses its
fangs to inject its victim with a
dose of venom. This paralyzes the
prey so it cannot move.

WEIRD OR WHAT?

Trapdoor spiders are among the
longest-lived spiders. Captive
ones can outlive pet dogs or even
cats. They have been known to
live beyond the age of 20!

Next the spider
injects the body with
digestive juices so the insides
turn to mush. Spiders' guts
are too narrow to cope
with solids.

LEAF-CURLING SPIDER

This web weaver uses a rolled-up leaf to make a secret hideaway, where predators and prey can't see it.

The spider fixes the leaf to the centre of its web. It stitches a seam to keep the leaf curled up, and sometimes lines the leaf with silk.

LEAF-CURLING SPIDER FACTS

SIZE: 1-cm-long body in females
(males are half the size)
HOME: woodlands and gardens
in Australia
EATS: flying insects

WEIRD OR WHAT?

If it can't find a leaf, a leaf-curling spider might fix a snail shell or a piece of paper to its web, and use that for its hideout instead!

Like many spider species, female leaf-curlers often eat their partner after mating. They may be cannibals, but they're good mums. They lay their eggs safe inside a curled-up nursery leaf, which they attach to a nearby plant.

Crab Spider

CRAB SPIDER FACTS

SIZE: 4- to 10-mm-long body
HOME: worldwide in gardens and woodlands
EATS: flies and bees

Crab spiders are masters of disguise. Their clever camouflage allows them to launch surprise attacks and ambush their prey.

This spider's pink body makes it hard to spot against the petals of a flower. It's waiting to catch a visiting insect.

This crab spider has the perfect disguise. Its splashy markings and lumpy body make it look just like fresh bird poo. No wonder it's called the bird dung crab spider!

WEIRD OR WHAT?

Some crab spider species are like chameleons. They can change colour to match the flower they are on!

Gotcha! This crab spider has ambushed a bee.

WHIP SPIDER

Whip spiders are not true spiders but they are arachnids.

They are named for their long front legs, which are used as sense organs. By waving these 'whips' around, the whip spider can locate prey.

WEIRD OR WHAT?

Young whip spiders use their whips another way – to stay in touch. They stretch them out to stroke their mum, brothers and sisters!

WHIP SPIDER FACTS

SIZE: body up to 45 mm long
HOME: worldwide in tropical and subtropical regions
EATS: arthropods, small lizards, frogs

Like their namesakes, wolf spiders are good hunters with excellent eyesight. They don't go out in packs, though. As adults they live and hunt alone.

WOLF SPIDER

WOLF SPIDER FACTS

SIZE: body ranges from 1 mm across to 3 cm (there are 2,300 species)

HOME: worldwide

EATS: insects, small arachnids

WEIRD OR WHAT?

A wolf spider mum frees her newly-hatched spiderlings from their egg sac by tearing it open with her fangs.

Wolf spiders are the most caring spider mums. The female carries her eggs around in a bag at the end of her body, next to her spinnerets.

ANT-MIMICKING SPIDER

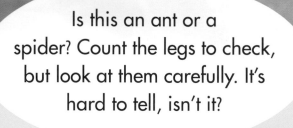

This ant mimic is a kind of jumping spider. It waves its long front legs in the air to look like an ant's antennae. Jumping spiders can leap several times their own body length.

Is this an ant or a spider? Count the legs to check, but look at them carefully. It's hard to tell, isn't it?

Spiders have two sneaky reasons for disguising themselves as ants. It puts off predators (because ants taste bitter and fight fiercely). And it's a way of getting close to ant prey.

This spider looks just like a red ant. It lives inside the ants' nest and preys on their eggs.

ANT-MIMICKING SPIDER FACTS

SIZE: around 8 mm long
HOME: worldwide in gardens, forests and fields
EATS: ants and other insects

The spider attacks its prey from behind so the ant can't cause too much damage while it's fighting back!

WEIRD OR WHAT?

Some ant mimics look like one species of ant when they are immature, and then another species when they are adult spiders!

GLOSSARY

antenna (plural antennae) One of a pair of feelers on an insect's head, used to smell, touch and hear.

aquatic Found in water.

arachnid An arthropod with eight legs. Spiders, scorpions, camel spiders (solifugids) and whip spiders (amblypygids) are all arachnids.

arthropod An animal with jointed legs and a body divided into segments covered by a hard outer skeleton (an exoskeleton). Arthropods include spiders, insects, centipedes, millipedes, crabs and lobsters.

camouflage Colours or patterns that help an animal to blend in to the surrounding environment.

cannibal An animal that eats others of its species.

class A term used by scientists to refer to a big group of living things that share certain characteristics. Arachnids, insects and mammals are all different classes.

crustacean An arthropod with two-parted legs. Crabs, prawns and woodlice are all crustaceans. Most crustaceans are aquatic.

gaucho A cowboy from the South American pampas (grasslands).

immobilize Make something unable to move.

invertebrate An animal that has no backbone. Some invertebrates, such as arthropods, protect their bodies with a hard outer skeleton, called an exoskeleton. They renew their exoskeleton as they grow by moulting. Some invertebrates, such as worms and jellyfish, have soft bodies.

larva (plural larvae) The young stage of an animal, usually an insect. The larva looks different to its adult form.

paralyze To make something unable to move.

pheromone A chemical or substance given off by an animal, usually in order to attract an animal of the same species.

predator An animal that hunts and kills other animals for food.

prey An animal that is hunted and killed by another animal for food.

repel Make something go away. Something that repels water is unwettable.

sac A thin-skinned bag. Spiders often protect their eggs in sacs of spun silk.

species One particular type of living thing. Members of the same species look similar and can reproduce together in the wild.

spinneret A spider's silk-producing organ, usually found at the base of its abdomen (the main part of its body). Some insect larvae, such as silkworms, also have spinnerets.

temperate From the two regions of the earth that lie between the equator and the poles, where the climate is warm in summer and cold in winter.

tropics The warm, wet parts of the world near to the equator (the imaginary line that circles the middle of the earth).

venom A chemical that is injected into another animal to paralyze it.

FURTHER INFORMATION

Books

Arachnids by Jan Beccaloni (Natural History Museum, 2009)

Buzz by Caroline Bingham (Dorling Kindersley, 2007)

Insiders: Insects and Spiders by Noel Tait (Templar, 2008)

Scary Creatures: Spiders and Minibeasts by Penny Clarke (Book House, 2003)

Spiders: The Ultimate Predators by Stephen Dalton (A&C Black Publishers, 2008)

DVDs

Animal Nation: Spiders (Pegasus Entertainment, 2007)

Killer Instinct: Spiders (Scanbox Entertainment, 2005)

Websites

American Arachnological Society
www.americanarachnology.org

BBC Wildlife Finder: Spiders
www.bbc.co.uk/nature/order/Spider

British Arachnological Society
www.britishspiders.org.uk

European Spiders Identification
www.eurospiders.com

INDEX